DATE DUE			

MONSTER HUNTING TODAY

MONSTER HUNTING TODAY

Daniel Cohen

Illustrated with photographs and prints

DODD, MEAD & COMPANY
NEW YORK

Copyright © 1983 by Daniel Cohen
All rights reserved
No part of this book may be reproduced in any form
without permission in writing from the publisher
Distributed in Canada by
McClelland and Steward Limited, Toronto
Manufactured in the United States of America

1 2 3 4 5 6 7 8 9 10

Library of Congress Cataloging in Publication Data

Cohen, Daniel.
  Monster hunting today.

  Includes index.
  Summary: Discusses the science of cryptozoology,
the study of hidden or unidentified animals, such as the
famous Loch Ness monster and Bigfoot, which many people
believe exist in remote parts of the world.
  1. Monsters—Juvenile literature. [1. Monsters.
2. Animals, Mythical] I. Title.
QL89.C626   1983   001.9′44   83-7496
ISBN 0-396-08184-3

84620

To all monster lovers

CONTENTS

MONSTER HUNTING TODAY

Introduction

WHAT, ANOTHER MONSTER BOOK?

Not just another monster book. A new one. The world of monsters does not stand still. New information comes in all the time. You may think you know about monsters. You probably do. But do you know what has been discovered lately? There have been more monster investigations in the past few years than ever before. Monster hunters have been everywhere — from the swamps of central Africa to the shores of Lake Champlain. To be up-to-date, you will want to know what these modern monster searchers have found.

First, a word about the word "monster." You won't find the vampire or the dragon in this book. Hardly anybody believes in vampires or dragons anymore. This is a book about animals that might *really* exist. They are called "monsters" mainly because they are large and mysterious, not because they are dangerous or frightening. Some of these creatures are not supposed to be dangerous or frightening at all. So, in a way, "monster" is not a very good word to describe them. It might be better to call them "unknown animals." But people have been calling such creatures "monsters" for a long time. Everyone knows what the Loch Ness monster is, or is supposed to be. If you said Loch Ness unknown animal, people wouldn't know what you were talking about. Let's stick to calling these things monsters.

And while we are on the subject of words, here is another one for you — *cryptozoology.* The first part of the word — *crypto* — comes from a Greek word meaning hidden or unknown. *Zoology* is the study of animals. So cryptozoology is the study of hidden or unknown animals. That's what this book is about.

The okapi is the last large land animal to be discovered. People once thought it was a myth. Now it is found in zoos all over the world.

Cryptozoology isn't a recognized branch of science — yet. You are not going to study it in school. But there are a few scientists who have done a lot of work in cryptozoology. They have led expeditions to remote and dangerous places. And they have used the most modern equipment available to try and snap a picture or find some other evidence that a strange and unknown animal really does exist.

Most people interested in cryptozoology are not scientists. But many of these "amateurs" have spent many years investigating the subject. They have become real experts.

Even the majority of scientists who don't believe in monsters treat cryptozoologists with new respect. These modern monster hunters are not just fooling around. They are making a serious and scientific attempt to find and identify unknown animals.

Early in 1982 a group of scientists and others got together to form the International Society of Cryptozoology. Members of the society come from all over the world.

The job for the cryptozoologist or modern monster hunter is not an easy one. No one is paid for monster hunting. Usually the investigations have to be carried out in the investigators' spare time. They spend their

Dr. Bernard Heuvelmans, the "father" of modern cryptozoology and president of the new International Society of Cryptozoology.

vacations chasing rumors of unknown animals. They can't even be sure the animal they are seeking really exists. Monster hunters usually have to spend their own money. Cryptozoology can be a very expensive hobby. There is never enough money. Modern monster searchers are always hard-pressed for funds. The largest modern searches have taken place at Loch Ness. But even at Loch Ness the searchers have never really had enough modern equipment. Fifty years of research at Loch Ness has cost less than a single space suit in the space shuttle program.

Don't think that just because the monster searchers have been short on money that they have not found anything. They certainly have, as you will soon see.

The modern search for monsters can be hard and frustrating, as well as expensive. It can also be uncomfortable and even dangerous. And the modern monster hunter sometimes runs the risk of being looked upon as a crazy person.

Why do people do it? There are lots of reasons. Most monster hunters would agree that one reason is the sheer adventure of the search.

Now let's see what they have found, and share the adventure.

1

THE DINOSAUR
THAT DIDN'T DIE

Dinosaurs were the largest land animals that ever lived. For over 140 million years they dominated the land masses of our planet. Then, about 65 million years ago, all the dinosaurs died out. No one knows why they died out. That's a real mystery. But no matter what the reason, they're all gone now. If we can be sure about one thing, it is that the dinosaurs are extinct.

Or are they?

Right now some of the most interesting monster hunting in the world is going on in the swamps of central Africa. A few dedicated researchers think that they have found evidence that a dinosaur — or something that appears to be a lot like a dinosaur — is alive and well in these swamps. The creature has been known under many names. But the name that is used most commonly now is *mokele-mbembe.*

The idea of a living dinosaur is not new. Around the year 1900 the British writer Sir Arthur Conan Doyle wrote a book called *The Lost World.* It was about a place that had not changed since the days of the dinosaurs. Conan Doyle's "lost world" was a land filled with dinosaurs. A lot of other writers of stories have used the same idea.

You have probably seen the movie *King Kong.* King Kong is a giant ape that lives on an island in the Pacific Ocean. Along with King Kong are a lot of other "prehistoric" creatures, including some dinosaurs.

So the idea that dinosaurs could still be alive somewhere has been a popular one — in fiction. But there were other kinds of stories about living dinosaurs. And these were supposed to be true. It was these supposedly true stories that gave Conan Doyle and others the ideas for their fiction.

Most of these supposedly true stories came out of central Africa. One hundred years ago parts of central Africa had not been thoroughly explored. It seemed possible that large and unknown animals could still live there.

One of those who told stories of strange creatures in the jungles and swamps was a traveler and adventurer nicknamed Trader Horn. Horn had a tale about something called the *jago-nini*. It was a giant lizard-like creature that lived in the swamps. Sometimes it came out of the water to eat people. Trader Horn had never seen the thing himself, but he had seen footprints. They were "about the size of a good frying pan around and had three claws instead of five."

Everyone agreed that old Trader Horn knew a lot about Africa. Everyone also agreed that old Trader Horn liked to tell a good story. Trader Horn didn't let truth get in the way of a good story.

But there were better and more truthful witnesses. One traveler in Africa said he saw a strange lizard-like creature floating down a flooded river on a log. The thing was at least 16 feet long. It was probably longer, but the witness couldn't tell. The creature's tail was in the water. The thing was all spotted and covered with scales.

An unknown giant lizard? No, said C.W. Hobley, the man who heard this story and wrote it down. The creature sounded more like some sort of dinosaur to Hobley. The survival of such animals, said Hobley, "is a thing to thrill the imagination of the scientific world." And not just the scientific world either. Everyone would be thrilled if a living dinosaur could be found.

Carl Hagenbeck collected African animals for zoos. He heard many stories of the unknown beast. He wanted to capture one to put on display in his own private zoo in Germany. Hagenbeck was sure that such a creature would be a great attraction. He sent out some of his agents to catch it. He offered

The most common belief is that mokele-mbembe is some sort of surviving dinosaur. Most descriptions make it sound like a small brontosaurus.

a huge reward for the animal. But he was always disappointed. Though lots of people reported seeing the thing, no one was ever able to catch it.

Still, Hagenbeck was sure that it was out there somewhere. "In the part of Africa where the animal is said to exist there are enormous swamps hundreds of square miles in extent. My travelers got very severe attacks of fever." That, Hagenbeck believed, was why the beast had never been captured.

Just before World War I a German

expedition to the Congo picked up stories of mokele-mbembe. Mokele-mbembe was described as being about the size of a small elephant. It had a long neck, a long tail, and smooth brownish-gray skin. It lived in big caves by the river. Sometimes it climbed on the river bank to eat plants that grew there. Mokele-mbembe was not dangerous. It only ate plants and was very shy.

Every time a monster becomes popular there seems to be a hoax. There were a lot of African dinosaur hoaxes. The most famous one was in 1919. Several newspapers in London, England, reported that some sort of a "monster" was running around the villages in central Africa tearing up huts and stomping on people.

The papers said this "monster" was a brontosaurus—a large type of dinosaur. The brontosaurus had a long neck, a small head, and a long tail. The descriptions of the "monster" did not make it sound like a brontosaurus—or anything else that had ever lived.

The stories were completely fantastic. They would not have been believed for a moment — except for one detail. The papers said that the Smithsonian Institution had sent an expedition to Africa to find the "monster." The Smithsonian Institution in Washington, D.C., really did have an expedition in central Africa at that moment. The stories said that the Smithsonian was offering a huge reward to anyone who could bring back the dinosaur.

All sorts of people said they were going to go to Africa to hunt the dinosaur. None of them ever did. Before long the Smithsonian Institution sent a letter to the London papers. The letter said the brontosaurus story was a fake.

Hoaxes can be very discouraging. But not all of the stories were obvious hoaxes. And stories of some sort of dinosaur-like creature in central Africa kept coming in. In 1976 an American reptile expert named James Powell heard some of these tales while he was working in Africa. He wanted to go looking for the creature. But he did not have the money to launch a real expedition. All he could do was collect more information about the creature.

When Powell got back to the United States he got in touch with America's leading cryptozoologist, Dr. Roy Mackal. Mackal had, of course, heard many of the old stories about the African dinosaur. Talking to Powell fired his enthusiasm to go looking for it. In early 1980 Powell and Mackal teamed up to make a quick expedition into the central African swamps.

The area in which the creature is most often reported is in the northern part of the Republic of the Congo. It is an area of over 50,000 square miles of swamp. And it is almost completely unexplored. There are no roads. There is practically no dry land. It is an awful region filled with bugs and snakes.

In 1980 Mackal and Powell never actually got into the area where the creature was reported. But they did talk to natives of the region. They said that they had either seen the creature or knew people who had seen it.

Many of those who live in or near the central African swamp are Pygmies. They live by hunting and fishing.

Several people reported that one of the creatures had been killed in an area around Lake Tele back in 1959. The animal was supposed to have been disturbing the fishermen. According to the stories, it had been killed with a spear. Then it was cut up. This turned out to be a hard job, because the creature was very large, and very tough. Then the flesh was cooked and eaten. The story ended with the information that everyone who had feasted on mokele-mbembe died. The flesh was supposed to be poisonous.

Mackal and Powell talked to a man named Nicolas Mondongo. He came from a village in the Likoula region where mokele-mbembe was well known. He said that his father had seen it many times. Nicholas Mondongo himself had seen the creature up close only once. He was in a canoe in a shallow river. The creature had been under the water. Mondongo didn't see it until he got quite close. Then the beast stood upright on its short legs. He could see the head and neck, its back, and part of its tail. The oddest thing about the creature was that it had a frill on the top of its head. The frill looked sort of like the comb of a rooster. Mondongo watched the strange animal for a few minutes. It made no move to attack, and did not look at all dangerous. Then it disappeared under the water again.

Mondongo estimated that the thing was over 30 feet long. Its long neck and head were about ten feet of the total length.

The description, except for the frill on the top of the head, made mokele-mbembe sound like a small brontosaurus. The brontosaurus was one of the largest dinosaurs ever to live. A big one might be over 200 feet long from nose to tail. However, smaller ones are known to have existed.

The accounts collected by Mackal and Powell were excellent. But stories, no matter how good they sound, are not hard evidence. More was needed, much more. The following year Dr. Roy Mackal went back to central

Searching for mokele-mbembe in the Congo. In the canoe are Richard Greenwell (left), secretary of the International Society of Cryptozoology, Dr. Roy Mackal, and Pastor Eugene Thomas.

Africa, with a larger expedition. Still, like most modern monster hunts, this expedition was not really large. There were only four Americans, including Mackal. And they didn't have a lot of money, or a lot of time. The Mackal expedition did get some support from the National Geographic Society.

The expedition got to Brazzaville, the capital of the Republic of the Congo late in October, 1981. Political conditions in that part of the world are very unstable. The government of the Republic of the Congo was very suspicious of foreigners. It took the members of the expedition days to get permission to fly to the interior. Much valuable time was wasted. Perhaps government officials didn't believe that they were really looking for dinosaurs.

Finally, after many frustrating delays, the group was allowed to fly 500 miles north to a mission at a place called Impfondo. From there they hoped to go by dugout canoe to the region in which mokele-mbembe had been seen. The expedition was now made up of the four American monster hunters plus an American missionary who had lived in the region for 26 years. There were also three Congolese army men, a Congolese biologist, and a number of Pygmy helpers.

From the start, progress in the canoe was

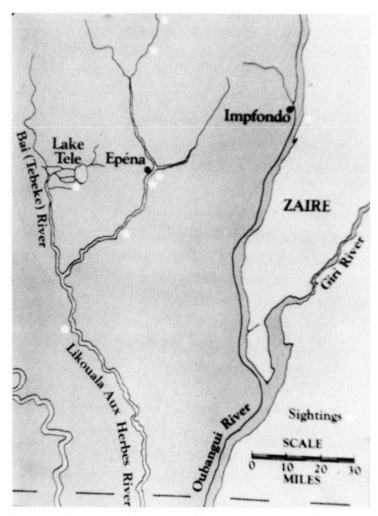

Map of the Congolese swamps in which the Mackal
expedition searched for mokele-mbembe. White stars
indicate spots where sightings of the creature have
been reported.

slow and difficult. The waterway was clogged with logs. An astonishing (and alarming) variety of snakes and insects dropped from the overhanging trees. The monster hunters got as far as the village of Kinami. There the expedition bogged down completely.

It was almost impossible to find a clear channel through the swamp. The original plan had been to go as far as Lake Tele. That was where mokele-mbembe had been reported most often. But at Kinami they made a disturbing discovery. The directions they had been given to Lake Tele were wrong. The lake could not be reached by water. The swamps between Kinami and the lake were completely impassable. They would have to walk through the swamp forest for days to reach the lake.

By this time the members of the expedition were exhausted. They were also running out of supplies and time. Sadly, they decided to abandon the project.

But all was not lost. The expedition did some exploring. And they saw things worth reporting. They found traces of what could have been a trail left by a large unkown animal. While paddling on the Likoula River some expedition members saw what they thought was a large animal submerge quickly in the water. It was too large for a crocodile. It might have been a hippopotamus. But no hippos are supposed to live in that area. So it might have been a large unknown animal. Perhaps it was mokele-mbembe itself.

And, of course, there were more stories from people who said that they had seen the monster of the swamps.

The trip back to the mission station was even worse then the trip out. The water level had dropped. The canoes kept running into underwater tree trunks. The snake population seemed to have gotten larger. The expedition members also got a number of tropical infections. These were very difficult to cure. Dr. Roy Mackal and his companions returned to America exhausted in mind and body.

The hunt for mokele-mbembe turned into a real old-fashioned jungle adventure. It was just like all those old jungle adventure movies.

Members of the Mackal expedition trekking through the snake-infested swamps of the Congo.

The hunt was followed by a controversy. One man who had originally been scheduled to go with the Mackal expedition had changed his mind. He formed his own expedition. The expedition consisted of the man and his wife.

They said that they actually reached Lake Tele by walking through the swamps. But that was just the beginning. They said that while at the lake they had seen mokele-mbembe.

And they said they had taken a picture of the beast.

The evidence sounds good. But it has turned out to be not nearly as good as it sounds. The only people who saw the monster were the man and his wife. The Congolese who had gone with them were not around when the creature made its appearance.

What about the photograph? People who have seen it say it isn't very clear. It is so fuzzy that it could be a picture of practically anything, taken practically anywhere.

The sighting and the picture got a lot of publicity. But they don't really prove anything. This sort of controversy is part of practically every modern monster hunt.

Meanwhile, out there in the swamps of Africa a survivor from the Age of the Dinosaurs may still remain to be discovered.

2

CHAMP, CHESSIE, AND OTHERS

Nessie of Loch Ness is the most famous freshwater monster in the world. It is probably the most famous monster of any kind in the world. And it should be. There is a lot of good evidence that such a creature really exists. But a couple of American freshwater monsters have become very famous in the past few years. One day Champ and Chessie may be as famous as old Nessie herself.

Champ is what people call the Lake Champlain monster. Champ just became widely known recently. But it is no Johnny-come-lately monster. Stories about a monster

Lake Champlain, home of Champ

in the lake have been around since before
Champlain was called Lake Champlain. The
first recorded sighting of the Lake Champlain
monster was made by the man after whom the
lake is named. He was the French explorer,
Samuel de Champlain.

Champlain first sailed into the lake in 1609.
Along with the usual wildlife, he saw
something that he had never seen before. It
was a snake-like creature about 20 feet long

The great showman, P.T. Barnum, offered a reward for Champ.

swimming in the lake. The thing had a head like a horse. Champlain had no idea what it was. Neither did anyone else.

From time to time a lot of other people have

spotted a large unknown creature, or monster, in Lake Champlain. During the nineteenth century, monster watching in Lake Champlain was a popular sport. The great showman P.T. Barnum offered $50,000 to anyone who could catch the creature. Barnum wanted to display it in his museum. But Barnum never had to pay a penny. No one ever delivered Champ to him.

Lake Champlain really is a pretty good place for a monster. It's big — 107 miles long and up to 14 miles wide. It's deep, 400 feet deep in some places. And it's cold. Most of the world's reports of lake monsters come from deep, cold, northern lakes just like Lake Champlain.

The lake lies in a valley between the Adirondack Mountains on the west and the Green Mountains to the east. For about 100 miles the lake marks the boundary between the states of New York and Vermont. A small portion of the lake is in Canada.

People who lived around the lake, or who came to vacation there, during the twentieth century were also interested in the monster.

Lake Champlain seen from Vermont's Button Island, the scene of many Champ sightings.

Practically every summer a few people reported seeing it. At least one boat owner ran regular monster-spotting cruises. But in general, the Lake Champlain monster was no big deal. It was only a local celebrity. And not much of a celebrity at that. It was very much in the shadow of more famous monsters like Nessie and Bigfoot.

In the world of monster hunting it only takes

a single dramatic event to turn an obscure local legend into a star. That is what happened with Champ.

On July 5, 1977, Sandra Mansi was standing on the shore in the northern part of Lake Champlain. She saw something moving in the water. At first she thought it was some fish just under the water. Then something that looked like a long neck topped by a small head broke through the surface of the lake.

"I was scared to death," Sandra Mansi said. "I had the feeling that I shouldn't be there."

Fortunately, she wasn't alone. It's not that she was in any danger. But her unsupported word would have meant nothing. Her future husband was with her. He too saw the thing with the long neck. Even more important was that she had her Kodak Instamatic camera with her. She snapped a picture of the thing in the water. That photo was the big breakthrough for Champ. But very few people knew it at the time.

When the picture was developed it showed what looked like the head, long neck, and part of the back of a creature coming out of the water. Sandra Mansi did not show her picture around at once. She was afraid that if she told people about it they would think that she was crazy. Or they would think that she was a faker. She would only show it to close friends.

Over the next couple of years there were a lot of monster-sighting reports in Lake Champlain. Sandra Mansi felt better. Now a lot more people believed in Champ. So she decided to make her picture public.

Quickly, the picture became famous. It was reprinted in such places as *Time* magazine and *The New York Times*.

Did the picture prove that Champ is real? Unfortunately, no. The picture is a pretty good one. It is in color. And it is fairly clear. But the Instamatic camera takes very small pictures. And the "monster" in the picture is smaller still. You can't see any details. The "head" of the creature is turned away from the camera. And it is in heavy shadows. No facial features can be seen. The thing in the picture looks like an unknown animal. But there is no way to be sure that it is a living creature at all.

There are other problems. Sandra Mansi says she is not exactly sure where she took the picture. Therefore, it is not possible to know how far away the object was. And if you don't know how far away it was, you can't estimate how big it was.

Finally, the whole thing could be a hoax. There have been a lot of hoaxes in the world of monster hunting. That possibility cannot be overlooked.

The Mansi picture was examined by several experts in photography. They said that as far as they could tell it was genuine. That is, the negative and the print had not been tampered with. But there was no way to prove that what had been photographed was really an animal, and if it was an animal, how big it was.

In August, 1981, a group of scientists, and nonscientists who are just interested in monsters, gathered in Burlington, Vermont, near Lake Champlain. They discussed Champ, and offered various theories.

Dr. Roy Mackal suggested that Champ

Some people think that Champ is a sea monster that looks like this.

might be a primitive, serpent-like whale called a zeuglodon (ZOO-glo-don). These creatures lived about 20 million years ago. Dr. Mackal believes that surviving zeuglodons may account for many of the monster sightings in cold northern lakes.

Others disagreed. Some thought Champ was a plesiosaur (PLEES-eo-sor). That is a large reptile that lived in the oceans during the time of the dinosaurs.

Still others suggested the possibility of a long-necked seal or otter. Most of those who met in Burlington, Vermont, couldn't guess what Champ was. Or even if Champ existed at all. But they wanted to find out.

If Champ does exist, people want to make sure it isn't harmed. The town of Port Henry, New York, which has become sort of a center for Champ watchers, took the lead. The town passed a law making the waters around the town off limits to people who want to "harm or harass" the lake monster.

On the Vermont side the state House of Representatives has been presented with a bill that makes it illegal to try and harm the creature. Whether it exists or not, Champ will have plenty of legal protection.

No one could be happier about all the Lake Champlain monster excitement than the people of the little town of Port Henry. They are busy selling Champ T-shirts and other monster souvenirs to tourists. Many visitors now come to the Lake Champlain area hoping to get a look at the famous monster.

Another North American water monster that has suddenly become famous is Chessie. Chessie is the name given to an unknown animal sighted in Chesapeake Bay.

Chesapeake Bay is an inlet of the Atlantic Ocean. The lower part of it is in the state of Virginia. The upper part is in Maryland. The bay is about 200 miles long and anywhere from four to 40 miles wide.

Since the bay is connected directly to the ocean, any monster in it is probably a sea monster that has just come near the shore.

People have been reporting a strange unknown creature in Chesapeake Bay for 50 years or so. No one kept any record of sightings from the early days. The first recorded sighting came in the summer of 1978. Some swimmers saw something they described as "grayish ... about 25 feet long ...swimming with a snake-like motion." Most of the reports of Chessie describe it as being from 25 to 35 feet long and very snake-like.

The most spectacular Chessie sighting took place on the morning of May 21, 1982. Robert and Karen Frew live in a house that overlooks the bay. On that day the Frews had some friends visiting. They looked out over the bay and saw a strange snake-like creature in the water about 200 feet away. Frew said the thing seemed to be about 35 feet long, and about one foot around. They could see the head and part of the body. The creature seemed to have humps, but Frew was not sure, because most of it stayed under the water.

Frew grabbed his binoculars to get a closer look. Then he had a better idea. He grabbed his videotape camera and took pictures. Frew kept his camera running for about three minutes. During that time the thing dived and came up several times.

There were some swimmers in the water. Frew and his wife called to them. The thing in the water dived down before it got too close to the swimmers. It surfaced on the other side of the swimmers. They never got a good look at it.

Those who have seen the videotape have all sorts of opinions about what it might show. Dr. Roy Mackal thinks that it supports his theory that many of the water monsters that have been reported are some form of the primitive whale, zeuglodon.

Harry Kristof, an underwater photographer who has worked at Loch Ness, has a very different opinion. He thinks the thing looks "like four kids swimming inside a plastic bag."

A group of scientists from the Smithsonian Institution met with the Frews and the other witnesses. They viewed the three-minute videotape. George Zug of the Smithsonian said that the tape was "most interesting." But he would not say whether he thought that the object in the picture was a real animal or not.

Others think that Chessie is some sort of huge water snake, or a gigantic eel. Says Robert Frew, "I want somebody to put a label on it." So far no one has. People are going to keep on trying.

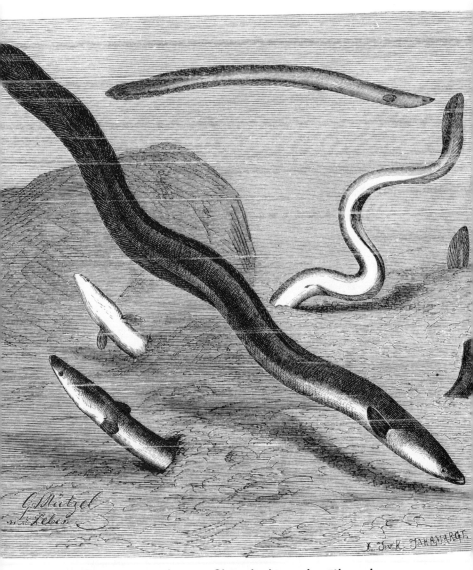

According to one theory, Chessie is a gigantic eel.

47

Before Champ and Chessie became popular, the best-known North American water monster was Ogopogo. Ogopogo is a creature that is supposed to live in Lake Okanagan in British Columbia. That's in the western part of Canada.

Like the home of so many other reported lake monsters, Okanagan is a large, deep, and cold body of water. The lake is 79 miles long, about two and a half miles wide, and up to 800 feet deep. The temperature of the water is usually around 34°F. That's just above freezing.

It's not the sort of lake that you would want to go swimming in. But for a very long time a lot of people have said that something large and unknown is swimming around in Lake Okanagan.

How about that name, Ogopogo? It sounds like an Indian name. But it isn't. The Indians who lived in the area did have a name for the creature. It was Natiaka. That meant lake monster or lake demon. When settlers began to move into the area they sometimes reported seeing the creature. At first they also called it Natiaka.

The funny name Ogopogo was pinned on the creature in the 1920s. It comes from an old British music hall song. It's just a nonsense word. Originally it had nothing to do with the lake monster. But somebody made up a song about the lake monster. In the song the thing was called Ogopogo. It is such a memorable name that it has stuck.

The creature is generally described as being anywhere form 30 to 70 feet long, with a snake-like body. Its head is like that of a horse or sheep. In a general sort of way this description fits in with that of other lake monsters.

Ogopogo has been famous longer than the Loch Ness monster. The Loch Ness monster did not become famous until the 1930s. Ogopogo has been well known since at least the 1920s. The town of Kelowna, British Columbia, on the shores of Lake Okanagan has put up a monument to the creature. Ogopogo is a geniune tourist attaction. The local people have a lot of fun with the stories.

There have been hundreds of sightings, some quite good. Still, Ogopogo has never attracted much serious attention from cryptozoologists. One possible reason is that there has never been a good, or well-publicized, photograph of the creature.

The closest thing to a good picture was taken in August, 1968. A man named Arthur Folden took about a minute of film of what he claimed was Ogopogo. By the time he got around to showing it to outsiders the film was already in pretty bad shape.

The object in the film that was supposed to be the monster was very unclear. Some people who saw the film thought it showed a living creature. Others thought it was a hoax, or a mistake. And they said so. Folden became very hurt and angry. He thought people were saying he was a hoaxer. Finally, he refused to show the film to anyone and would say nothing more on the subject of Ogopogo.

The monster of Lake Okanagan continues to be seen. There are a few sightings reported every year, usually during the summer months. Perhaps one day soon something will happen to bring this North American water monster the fame that it has missed so far.

3

THE GIANT OCTOPUS

Not all modern monster searches take place in the jungle. Or in the forests, or high mountains. Not all monster searches take place outdoors. Sometimes the search takes place in the dusty basements of museums. Or in libraries among piles of old books and newspaper articles.

That is what happened in the case of the giant octopus. It is an amazing story. And it is an important one. The giant octopus is the only unknown animal for which we have physical evidence. The giant octopus is also a huge and frightening-looking creature. A real monster.

The story, at least the modern part of it, began in 1957. F.G. Wood is a scientist who was working for the U.S. Navy in Florida. He ran across an old newspaper clipping with the headline "Facts About Florida." It was a short item about the remains of a gigantic octopus that had been washed ashore on the beach at St. Augustine, Florida, late in November, 1896.

The octopus has a round body. Coming out of the body are eight tentacles. The largest *known* octopus lives in the Mediterranean. It can measure 25 feet across. That is from the tip of one tentacle to the tip of the tentacle on the opposite side of its body. That's pretty big. You wouldn't want to meet one while swimming. But it is just a little tiny thing compared to the octopus described in the article. That octopus was supposed to be 200 feet across! If you laid the thing out on a football field with the tip of one tentacle touching the goal line, the tip of the opposite tentacle would reach two-thirds of the way to the opposite goal line. Other tentacles would reach right into the stands. A 200-foot octopus

would be the largest invertebrate — that is an animal without a backbone — in the world.

Wood was amazed by the article. He had never heard of such a creature. If such a creature existed it would be a real monster. But did it exist? Newspapers have often printed little items about this or that "monster" found washed up somewhere. Usually these stories turned out to be mistakes. When investigated, the "monster" is found to be a dead whale or shark. Sometimes the stories turned out to be hoaxes. That might be the case with this story too. Besides, it had happened a long time ago.

Still, Wood decided to try and check it out. He had two reasons for this. First, he was working not far from where the creature was supposed to have been washed ashore. Second, the article mentioned a name that he knew. The article said that the identification of

The largest known octopus is only 25 feet across. The giant at St. Augustine may have been as much as 200 feet across.

the giant octopus had been approved by Professor A.E. Verrell of Yale University. Verrell, of course, had been dead a long time. But his name was still well known among people who know about sea animals. In his day Professor Verrell had been the world's best-known authority on the octopus and squid. He was particularly famous for his study of the giant squid.

The squid is a close relative of the octopus. But it doesn't look too much like an octopus. The squid has a long torpedo shape. Its head and all its tentacles are at one end. Small squids had always been known. The sea is full of them. For centuries there had been rumors that some squids grew to gigantic sizes. Most scientists didn't believe the rumors. There were reports of giant squids being washed ashore. Usually the remains disappeared before scientists had a chance to look at them.

However, by the middle of the last century the evidence had piled up. The scientific world finally accepted the existence of the giant squid. The largest known giant squid was 55

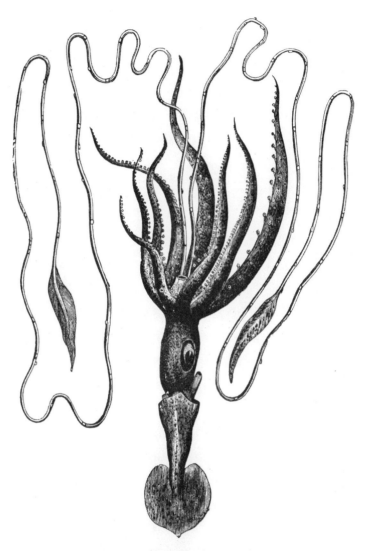

The squid, a close relative of the octopus, can grow
to gigantic size.

feet from tip of tail to tip of tentacles. But a lot of people believed that squids could grow much larger. And the scientist who knew more about giant squids than anyone else was A.E. Verrell. If Verrell had examined the giant octopus, why had Wood never heard of it? That was a mystery.

So Wood began writing letters and checking libraries. It turned out that there was a lot of information on the subject of the giant octopus still around. People had just forgotten about it. No one had looked at the information for fifty years. The basic facts related in the newspaper article were true.

Here is what had happened. On November 30, 1896, two boys had been riding their bikes along the beach at St. Augustine. There had been a storm not long before. A lot of strange things had been washed up on the beach. The strangest and largest thing was a pinkish mass, that had been half-buried in the sand. It looked like the rotting remains of a once-living creature. But the creature must have been huge. What kind of creature had it been?

Photograph of the remains washed ashore at St. Augustine, Florida, in 1896.

There was no way for the boys to know. The mass was shapeless. It had been badly battered by the sea.

The boys told everyone about their find. One of the people who heard the story was Dr. DeWitt Webb. Webb was a medical doctor. He also had an interest in natural science. In fact, Webb was founder and president of the local Institute of Science. Dr. Webb was the closest thing to a scientist in St. Augustine in 1896. Naturally, he was interested in the boys' find.

Webb went down to the beach to examine the mass himself. At first he thought it must be the remains of a whale. A whale was the only creature that he could think of that was large enough to leave such remains. But the more he looked at the remains the more he became convinced that it wasn't a whale. He became convinced that the remains were those of a giant octopus.

Now Webb knew about the giant squid. And he knew that the octopus is a close relative of the squid. Since there was a giant squid, why not a giant octopus as well? Others had suggested such a possibility. But there was no evidence to support suggestions. The remains on the beach might be the evidence.

Webb took some photographs of the mass. And he set some people to digging it out of the sand. One of the diggers, a man named Wilson, said that he found the partial remains of some of the octopus's gigantic arms buried near the main part of the body.

Another view of the gigantic remains at St. Augustine

Unfortunately, before the mass was completely dug out of the sand there was another storm. The mass was washed out to sea again. It was thrown back on the beach two miles south of its original landing place. Now it was in even worse shape than it had been before. The arms, if any, had completely disappeared.

Webb was still sure that the mass was the remains of an unknown, but gigantic, octopus. He knew that he was no expert. So he decided to contact the number one expert, Dr. Verrell at Yale University in Connecticut. He sent Verrell a report on what he had found. He also sent copies of the pictures that he had taken.

Verrell at first thought that the mass was the remains of a giant squid. But the more information he got, the more he came around to Webb's belief that the thing was a giant octopus. He even wrote an article for a scientific magazine on the subject. One thing Verrell did not do was go to Florida to examine the thing in person. In 1898 the trip between Connecticut and Florida took a long time. Verrell never could find the time. Nor did any other known scientist make the trip to examine the mass on the beach. That was a real shame. Webb was the only person to give a firsthand account of the find.

Webb was worried that another storm would wash the remains away forever. He had a team of horses drag the mass away from the edge of the water. That didn't help much. In March there was another storm. The mass was washed out to sea again. It was washed up at a new spot on the beach once again. It was in even worse shape. Then still another storm took it out to sea forever. So what may have been the most remarkable animal discovery of modern times just vanished.

But before the remains had disappeared forever Webb had cut off a few pieces. He packed them in a preservative solution and shipped them off to Verrell at Yale. Webb sent another batch of pieces to what is now the Smithsonian Institution in Washington, D.C.

When Verrell got the pieces that Webb sent him he was very disappointed. To him they looked like pieces of whale blubber. So he changed his mind and decided that the thing on the beach was the remains of a whale. A number of other scientists who looked at the pieces also decided that they were from a whale. The rotting remains of a whale are not that unusual. The only problem was that those scientists who decided that the remains were from a whale had never actually been to Florida to see the remains. They made their judgment from pieces. And they do not seem

The man standing next to the remains is probably Dr. DeWitt Webb.

to have looked at the pieces very closely.

The man who had sent the remains—Webb—was amazed by Verrell's change. He

64

sent the professor letter after letter protesting. But Verrell would not change his mind again. He said it was a whale, and most people agreed with him. And so the matter dropped. The opinion of an unknown Florida doctor could not stand against the opinion of a distinguished expert like Professor Verrell of Yale. Everybody forgot about the mass on the beach.

At some point a Florida newspaperman must have run across the story. He included it in the "Facts About Florida" column. But he only knew, or only used, half the story. He did not include Verrell's final opinion — that the remains were those of a whale.

When F.G. Wood began investigating the case in 1957 he found a lot of information. The letters that Webb had sent to Verrell were still on file at Yale. So were some of the photographs. The first photos that Webb had taken had somehow been lost. But drawings made from the photos were found. And there were some photographs taken after the mass had been washed ashore a second time. They didn't show much detail. They did show that something huge and strange-looking had been washed up on the beach.

After looking at all of the evidence, Wood was not sure that Verrell's final opinion was correct. The thing just didn't look like the remains of a whale. If he could find the pieces of the mass that Webb had sent to Verrell that might settle the question. But in the more than fifty years since they had been sent they had vanished from Yale.

Then Wood remembered that Webb had sent pieces of the mass to two places. One was Yale and the other was the Smithsonian Institution. The Smithsonian Institution is America's national museum. It has sometimes been called "America's attic." All sorts of things are collected there. The Smithsonian is famous for not throwing things away. Perhaps the specimens might still be there in some dusty corner, Wood thought.

Wood called on a friend, Dr. Joseph F. Gennaro of the University of Florida. Gennaro had contacts at the Smithsonian. Sure enough, when they checked among the thousands of jars of preserved specimens of ocean creatures they found one labeled *Verrell's Giant Octopus.* The Smithsonian apparently never heard of Verrell's change of mind. In any case, they never changed the label. That was a good thing, because without that label the specimens never would have been found. They didn't look at all special.

Gennaro went to Washington personally to pick up some samples. Inside a very large container were half a dozen large chunks of whitish material. They were floating around in a preserving solution. Gennaro cut off a few pieces to study in his own laboratory. The material turned out to be very tough and hard to cut. It was also in very bad shape. It didn't look like much of anything. But when Gennaro put a small sample under the microscope he was sure of one thing. The sample had not come from a whale. It had come from either a squid or an octopus. Further tests revealed that the sample had come from an octopus. The old Florida doctor had been right all along. Gennaro called the find "fantastic."

Can we say that without a doubt the giant

octopus exists? Not quite. The samples that Gennaro examined under his microscope were over fifty years old. And they were very much decayed. Mistakes can be made. What we need is the remains of another giant octopus to be washed up somewhere. That would be real proof. But that hasn't happened yet. Why not?

The reason could be that the giant octopus is very rare. And that it lives on the ocean bottom. The chance that such a creature would be washed ashore is slight indeed.

But there are rumors of such a creature. Wood had once worked in the Bahama Islands. He had heard some of the guides and fishermen talk about the giant octopus that lived in the deep water around the islands.

One person told Wood a story. He said that when he was a boy he and his father went fishing in the deep water. His father hooked onto something very heavy. As he pulled the line up, his father found that a giant octopus had grabbed hold of it. The creature was no 200 feet across. But it was an awful lot bigger than any octopus should be. As it neared the surface the octopus let go of the line and disappeared into the deep water.

The stories about a species of giant octopus living off the Bahamas fitted in with what happened in Florida in 1896. A strong ocean current sweeps past the Bahamas and brushes the coast of Florida. If one of the deep-water giants was caught in the current it might easily be carried to Florida.

Today, scientists have equipment that allows them to explore deep into the ocean. Someday soon underwater explorers may catch a glimpse of one of these giants scuttling across the ocean floor. Or, just by chance, the remains of one may be washed ashore somewhere. That may happen tomorrow. Or next year, or ten years from now. When the remains of another giant octopus are found, that will be big news.

4

THE SEARCH AT
LOCH NESS

People have been searching for Nessie, the Loch Ness monster, for over half a century. The Loch Ness monster has been more thoroughly investigated than any other unknown animal in the world. Many of the most important discoveries have been made over the last few years. We are going to look at these recent discoveries.

But first, let's back up for a moment. There just may be a few of you who don't know the history of the Loch Ness monster.

Loch Ness is a long lake in northern Scotland. Loch is the Scottish word for lake.

The ruins of Urquhart Castle stand alongside the deepest part of the loch. This is where Nessie is sighted most often.

Loch Ness is about 24 miles long and about a mile wide. The water is very deep — 800 feet or more at some points. The water is also very cold, and very dark. The water is dark because there is a lot of vegetable material in it. Even a strong light will penetrate only about 15 feet into the dark water. That's important to remember.

There have been tales of a monster in the loch for centuries. There are tales of monsters in other Scottish lochs too. And there are tales of monsters in Irish lakes. In fact, there are tales of monsters in lakes all over the world.

Monster stories can be a lot of fun. But they are not proof that an unknown animal exists. The real hunt for the Loch Ness monster began during the 1930s. That was when a road was built around the loch. Before that, Loch Ness had been very isolated. The road builders cut down a lot of trees and people could get a better look at the water.

Interest in the Loch Ness monster moves in jumps. Something exciting will happen, and there will be a jump in interest. Then people will forget about Nessie for a while. Then something else interesting will happen and there will be another jump.

The first big jump came in 1933 when a local newspaper printed an article about a couple that had seen a "monster" in the water. There was another big jump in 1934. That was when

Headquarters for one of the many Loch Ness monster expeditions that have taken place over the years.

a picture of what is supposed to be the Loch Ness monster was taken. The picture shows what appears to be the long neck and small head of a creature sticking out of the water. That is the most famous monster picture in the world. The photo really sparked interest in the subject. Then World War II came along. People had a lot of other problems on their minds.

After the war people began drifting back to Loch Ness to look for the monster. All sorts of people reported that they had seen "something" in the loch. The first really important postwar event took place on April 23, 1960.

A lone monster hunter named Tim Dinsdale shot a brief film of what he thought was the monster. The "monster" was a long way from Dinsdale when he shot his film. The film runs about four minutes. It is not much to look at. All you can see is a little spot moving across the water. Yet Dinsdale was sure that he had something important. He gave his film to photo experts in the Royal Air Force. They examined the film closely. Finally they decided that the object in the film was probably a living creature. And a large one.

That news stirred up a lot of interest. People who had never believed in the Loch Ness monster before suddenly began to wonder if there might not be something to it after all.

Up until the late 1960s, practically all of the investigation at Loch Ness had been done by individuals. Tim Dinsdale was all alone when he made his film. He could only afford to stay for six days, and shot his famous film on the last day. His camera equipment was not the best available. Solitary monster hunters are always short of funds.

During the late 1960s, however, things began to change. Groups were organized to look for the Loch Ness monster. Some of the groups could afford to use modern equipment. Some of the monster-hunting groups at Loch Ness began using sonar.

Sonar is very useful at Loch Ness. If the monster exists, it spends most of its time underwater. So that's the best place to look for it. But, as I said, the water is dark, and cold. Divers can't stay underwater for long. Even with a strong light a diver can't see very far anyway.

Sonar allows searchers to "see" in the dark waters of the loch. Sonar works underwater the same way radar works in the air. Both allow people to detect objects without the use of light. The sonar equipment sends out a

Tourists and monster hunters share a platform at Loch Ness.

burst of sound. If the sound hits something, it bounces off the object like an echo. Sonar is sometimes called "echo location."

Sonar is used by navies around the world to locate submarines and other underwater targets. And during the 1960s sonar was used by monster hunters to try and locate the Loch Ness monster. Sometimes the sonar equipment was put in a boat that cruised around the loch. Other times the equipment was placed at the edge of the water. The monster hunters tried to pick a spot where they thought the monster might pass by.

A team of scientists from the University of Birmingham in England used shore-based sonar equipment. Several times their equipment picked up echoes of what the scientists believe was the Loch Ness monster. In fact, these results indicate there are several large unknown animals in Loch Ness. At one point the sonar tracked a group of from five to eight large unknown creatures swimming together.

Actually, the name Loch Ness *monster* is a bit confusing. That sounds as if there is only one monster. But there can be no single monster that is hundreds of years old. Scientists who believe in the creature know that there has to be more than one. There must be a group or herd of unknown animals in the loch. They are born in the loch, grow up and breed there. And they die in the loch too.

The University of Birmingham sonar findings offered strong support for this theory. Some scientists believe sonar has provided the most important evidence for the Loch Ness monster.

But for the nonscientist, sonar isn't very dramatic. The results are technical and hard to understand. To the average person the records of a sonar contact don't look like a monster or anything else. We just have to take some expert's word for the fact that the sonar did locate a group of large unknown animals. Photographs, particularly close-up photographs, are different. Everybody can look at a photograph. They can decide for themselves whether the thing in the photo looks like a monster or not.

Over the years there have been a lot of photographs and films taken of what is supposed to be the Loch Ness monster. I have mentioned only a couple of them. However, all of those photographs were taken on the

The south end of Loch Ness on a calm day. Monster sightings are usually made under calm conditions.

surface. But the creature spends most of its time underwater. The best place to take a picture of it should be underwater. But taking underwater pictures at Loch Ness presents all sorts of problems.

The biggest problem is the dark water. Even if you put a strong light on a camera, the object to be photographed has to be pretty close. It has to come within 15 feet or less of the camera. A photographer on the shore can spend days, weeks, months, or even years waiting for the monster to appear. A photographer can't spend years or even days underwater waiting for the monster to get close enough to take its picture.

You can put an automatic camera underwater. But how would the camera know when to snap a picture? An American scientist, Dr. Robert Rines of the Academy of Applied Science, came up with one solution to the underwater photography problem. He attached an automatic underwater camera to sonar equipment. The sonar operated all the time. When the sonar picked up signs of a large object moving nearby it triggered the camera. The camera would then automatically begin taking pictures. In that way Dr. Rines hoped that he would be able to get a photograph of the large object detected by the sonar. And he hoped that large object would be the Loch Ness monster.

The system sounds easy. It's not. Sometimes the sonar failed to work properly. Other times it was the camera that didn't work. Often the camera seemed pointed in the wrong direction, and didn't get a picture of anything. All too often the object was too far away from the camera to show up on the film. It was all very frustrating.

Then on August 8, 1972, everything worked. Dr. Rines's underwater camera took two of the most spectacular photos ever of the Loch Ness monster. Or what he assumed was the Loch Ness monster. Many regard these two photos as the best photographic evidence for the existence of the monster.

The camera took two pictures of what appears to be a diamond-shaped flipper, and part of the rounded body of a large unknown animal swimming in the murky waters of Loch Ness.

How big is the animal? It's not possible to tell. Most of those who have studied the pictures, and the conditions under which they were taken, estimate that the flipper alone is four to six feet long. Any creature that has such a flipper could be really huge. But we can't be sure of the size.

The photographs appeared in magazines

The ancient marine reptile known as a plesiosaur (shown in background) is still the most popular candidate for the Loch Ness monster. But many other animals have also been suggested.

and newspapers all over the world. They also appeared in leading scientific journals. In the past some scientists suspected that many Loch Ness monster photos were faked. No one ever accused Dr. Rines of faking these photos.

The two "diamond-shaped flipper" photographs produced another one of those jumps of interest in Loch Ness monster investigation. More and more people came to the loch to look for the monster. Different organizations offered to help pay for expeditions to search for the Loch Ness monster.

In 1975 Dr. Robert Rines came back to Loch Ness. He had an improved version of his underwater camera-sonar equipment. He had several cameras this time. Once again he got some spectacular pictures.

A picture taken on June 20, 1975, shows what looks like a creature with a very long neck swimming in the distance. Eight hours later something seems to have actually bumped into the same camera. The bump sent the camera rocking back and forth. One moment it was pointed upward and took a picture of the bottom of the boat from which it was suspended. Next it took a picture of what might be the rough hide of an animal swimming nearby. The next photo shows what might be the head of a truly monstrous-looking animal.

Note that I said "might be." The pictures are

not very clear. They might also show a piece of a strangely shaped log. There is no way of telling for sure. But even with the uncertainty, these photos created more excitement than ever before. It looked as if the search at Loch Ness was finally beginning to pay off. Through the use of modern scientific equipment the Loch Ness monster would finally be identified.

The biggest Loch Ness monster expedition ever was launched in 1977. All sorts of advanced scientific equipment was brought to the loch. There were more scientists and technicians gathered there than ever before in history. If any expedition should have produced the final evidence that would prove the monster exists, this was it. Yet the expedition came up with practically nothing in the way of evidence. There were a few interesting sonar readings. But they were not nearly as good as those made years before by the University of Birmingham team. There were no worthwhile pictures at all. Once again the Loch Ness monster escaped detection.

That's the way it has always been with

Nessie. Just when the final, absolute proof seems at hand, it slips away. The monster remains what it has always been — a mystery.

The elusiveness of the monster has led some to the sad conclusion that there is no Loch Ness monster. In 1982 a Scottish engineer named Robert Craig suggested that monster sightings and photographs have been caused by logs. Craig said that the logs come from a particular type of pine tree that grows on the shores of the loch. These logs can be preserved in water for a very long time. Craig thinks that gas formed in the loch sometimes pushes such logs to the surface. Lumps of resin on a log give it the appearance of having a snout or fins. Craig's theory was printed in a leading British scientific publication. It was also picked up by newspapers all over the world.

Another doubter is the British naturalist, Dr. Maurice Burton. Burton once believed in the Loch Ness monster. But after studying the evidence for years he became discouraged. He now thinks that otters which live in the loch have created most of the monster excitement. Burton says, "Where two or more family parties of otters swim behind the other, they resemble the coils of a huge sea serpent." Sometimes the lead otter will rear up out of the water to see what is going on. In that way it can look like "the head and neck of a serpent." Burton also says the loch may contain really huge otters, up to eight feet long. An eight-foot otter in Loch Ness would not really be a monster. But it certainly would be an unexpected animal.

None of these skeptical theories are completely new. In one form or another they have been around for years. They are as impossible to prove or disprove as the existence of the monster itself. Cryptozoologists admit that some sightings and some photos may be explained by logs and otters or other non-monstrous things. But they say that not all of the evidence can be accounted for in this way. They say there must be something else. A real unknown animal. A real monster.

After the disappointment of 1977, worldwide

interest in the monster slipped. It was no longer big news. But that does not mean that dedicated monster hunters have given up on it. Not at all. Every year they come back to the loch with their cameras and binoculars, hoping to catch a glimpse of the creature.

The monster hunters always have a new plan, a new scheme. Some have drawn fancy plans for a trap to catch the monster. The trap has never been built. It probably never will be built. No one can be sure that a trap would not hurt the creature. It's against the law to hurt the Loch Ness monster.

There was a plan to train dolphins to swim around the loch looking for the monster. That plan never worked out.

Miniature submarines have been used from time to time. They proved to be expensive to operate. Besides, they didn't work very well.

In June, 1982, one of the Goodyear blimps was brought from Rome to Loch Ness to aid in the search. Monster hunter Tim Dinsdale with his cameras was on board. The blimp cruised back and forth over the loch for a week. The weather was poor. There was a lot of wind and mist, so nothing was seen.

The Goodyear blimp went back to Rome. But Dinsdale still believes that a small blimp would be very practical for keeping a large area of the loch under observation for a long time.

So, despite disappointment and frustrations, the search at Loch Ness goes on. The monster hunters are not discouraged. They say that with the photographs, the sonar, and the thousands upon thousands of sightings by responsible people, there is already more than enough evidence to be sure that the Loch Ness monster exists. It is only a matter of time, they say, before the searchers get close enough, and lucky enough, to figure out exactly what kind of animal it is.

Someday the monster hunters may be proven right. You may be around to see pictures of the real Nessie, the Loch Ness monster.

5

THE ALMA AND OTHER WILDMEN

You have surely heard about Bigfoot. You have probably also heard about the Yeti or Abominable Snowman. That is a hairy two-legged creature that is supposed to live in the mountains of Tibet.

But did you know that stories about the same sort of creatures come from all over the world? Over the past few years the stories have been attracting a lot of attention from cryptozoologists.

In the Soviet Union the creature is called the Alma. And some Soviet scientists are looking for it right now.

The Soviet Union is a huge country. It has the largest land area of any country in the world. Large parts of the country are still wild and not many people live there. It is from such areas that stories of the "wildman" come.

Tribesmen who live in or near the mountains of the eastern part of the Soviet Union tell stories of a shaggy "wildman." The creature is supposed to be human, or nearly so. It lives in the mountains and other remote places. It sometimes raids farms and gardens for food. But usually the wildman stays away from people. The tribesmen consider the creature harmless. It is called by many names. The most common name is the Alma.

Stories about strange creatures are always coming out of remote places. Scientists in the Soviet Union and elsewhere don't usually pay much attention to such stories. They didn't take stories of the Alma seriously either, until 1957. Then they got a report they could not ignore. The report didn't come from a simple tribesman or an uneducated peasant. It came from a scientist. He said he had seen the creature at close range.

The scientist-witness was Alexander G. Pronin. He was a specialist in water resources. In August, 1957, Pronin and a team of other scientists were in the Pamir Mountains. The Pamir Mountains are in the eastern part of the Soviet Union, near China. Very few people live in the region. Most of those who do are nomads — people who have no permanent home, but move from place to place. No one listened to their stories about the Almas they saw.

Some important river systems begin in the Pamir Mountains. Pronin and the other scientists were sent there to study the water supply.

At noon on August 12, 1957, Pronin was walking along a river valley. He looked up and there was what he called a "strange sight." A figure was moving across the snow a few hundred feet up the valley. The figure looked almost — but not quite — human. It was hunched over, and it had very long arms. The arms dangled almost down to the creature's knees. Strangest of all, the figure was completely covered with reddish-gray hair. Pronin

The Himalayan sloth bear has often been mistaken for
Abominable Snowman types of creatures.

was astonished. He just stood and watched the figure for about five minutes. Then it walked behind a large rock. He couldn't see it anymore. Pronin did not try to follow the figure.

Three days later Pronin saw the figure again. This time it was farther away and harder to see. But he had no doubt that it was the same creature he had seen before.

Now he became very curious about what he had seen. He asked some of the people who lived in the area. They weren't surprised. They weren't even interested. Their reaction was, "Oh, it's just one of the wildmen."

The people of the Pamirs didn't worry about the wildmen. They could be a nuisance sometimes. They would steal pots or other household items when they could. Later these items might be found high in the mountains. But the wildmen certainly were not dangerous. They weren't exactly common, people said. But then they weren't really rare either. The local people just didn't think they were worth fussing about. Besides, outsiders usually didn't believe the stories anyway.

While Pronin was asking people about the wildmen, one of the expedition's rubber boats disappeared. Later the boat was found miles upstream. There was no way the boat could have drifted upstream. Someone had to pull it there. Someone, or something. The people said that was just the sort of thing a wildman would do. It was like stealing a cooking pot and then leaving it in the mountains. Pronin also thought that was what a wildman would do.

When Pronin told his story to other scientists, some didn't believe him. They thought he was seeing things that were not there. Or that he was just making a joke. Pronin came in for a lot of kidding about his wildmen tale. He didn't think it was one bit funny. He was pretty angry and bitter at people who made jokes about the story.

But not all Soviet scientists refused to take him seriously. Professor Jeanne Kofman led several expeditions to find the wildman. She was checking out reports of the strange being that had come from mountainous areas in several different parts of the Soviet Union. Professor Kofman never found the wildman herself. It was not seen by any of the members of her research team. But they did collect accounts from over 300 people who said that they had seen the creature. Some members of the team found large, human-like footprints. They found pieces of food, like corncobs, that looked as if they had been chewed by the creature. They even found places where they thought the wildman had spent the night. But they never found the creature itself.

The biggest Soviet supporter of the wildman, or Alma, as he prefers to call it, is not a scientist but a historian. His name is Professor Boris Porshnev. Even before Pronin told his story, Professor Porshnev had been collecting stories about the Alma. After Pronin's sighting became known a lot more people in the Soviet Union became interested in the Alma. Naturally, they turned to Porshnev for more information. He knew more about the Alma than anyone else.

Professor Boris Porshnev, Soviet expert on the Alma.

Porshnev became head of a Soviet scientific committee on the Alma. He has written books and papers on the subject. He has given lectures all over the country. Many scientists don't believe him. But some think that he may have something, that there may really be such a creature.

Here is the sort of account that Pronin has collected. It comes from the far eastern part of the Soviet Union.

There were two travelers who were led into the mountains by a local herdsman. One morning they saw a strange figure standing near the horses. They thought it was someone who was trying to steal the horses. They ran after the figure. It could not run very fast. They caught the "horse thief" easily. Much to their surprise they found that what they had caught was not human.

It was about the height of an average man, but it was completely covered with hair. Its face was ape-like. Its feet were very large for its size.

The creature did not seem dangerous. In fact, it seemed scared. All it could do was make squeaking noises. When the local herdsman came to look, he just shrugged. "It's just a wildman," he told them. "There are a lot of them around here. They don't hurt anybody."

The travelers decided to let their captive go free. But they followed it. They found that it lived in sort of a cave. Inside the cave was a bed made of straw and grass.

Those Soviets who believe in the Alma do

The orangutan was called the "wild man of the woods."

not think that it is an ape. They think it really is some sort of wild *man*. Perhaps it is some very primitive type of human that was once common, but now has become very rare. It only lives in mountainous areas and other hard-to-reach places.

The attitude of Soviet scientists toward the Alma is a lot like the attitude of American scientists toward Bigfoot. They don't believe that there is enough evidence to say that such a creature really exists. But they are not willing to completely write off the possibility either. While there is no major Soviet effort to find the Alma, expeditions do, from time to time, search for it.

The Alma has also attracted the attention of some Western scientists. Dr. Myra Schackley, a respected British archaeologist, thinks that the Almas are some sort of prehistoric human or caveman. The best possibility, says Schackley, is Neanderthal man. During the Ice Age the Neanderthal man was common in Europe. But Neanderthals disappeared. No one knows why.

Artist's drawing of a Neanderthal family. Some people believe that the Alma and other wildmen may be surviving Neanderthals.

Dr. Schackley thinks some Neanderthals survived by retreating to desolate places. These survivors, she says, are now called Almas. Schackley was on an expedition to Outer Mongolia. She found stone tools that looked as if they had been made by

Neanderthals. The herdsmen who lived in the area said they had been made by the Almas who once lived there.

The herdsmen also said that all the Almas now lived in caves high in the mountains. They seemed surprised that anyone was interested in the Almas. Or that anyone might doubt that they exist.

Most Western scientists still doubt that they exist. But Schackley's theory was published in a leading scientific journal. That means that scientists are now prepared to take the idea of the Alma a bit more seriously.

China also has its wildman stories.

Now that may seem surprising because wildman stories usually come from places where few people live. China is the most heavily populated country in the world. The Chinese try to use every last bit of their land because there are so many Chinese. But there are still dense forest regions in northern China in which few people live. It is from such regions that stories of the Chinese wildman come.

Probably the most amazing account was that of a man called Wang Zelin. Wang had gone to a museum with some friends. They stopped at an exhibit on primitive man. One of the items in the exhibit was a plaster statue of Peking man. Peking man is a very primitive type of human that had lived in China over a million years ago. Peking man is much more primitive then Neanderthal man. Wang stared at the plaster statue. His friends could not drag him away. He pointed to it and said, "I saw one of those."

Then Wang told his story.

It was in the 1940s. China was at war. Wang was a soldier. He had been sent to a remote northern area. There had been no fighting in that area in a long time. Wang was astonished, and a bit frightened, when he suddenly heard gunshots.

He went to the place from which the gunshots had come. He found a crowd of people surrounding a corpse. But it wasn't a human corpse. Local people said it was a wildman.

The corpse had a face like the one of the model of Peking man that Wang had seen in the museum. "The face was narrow with deep-set eyes, while the cheekbones and lips jutted out." It was fairly tall and the whole figure was covered by a coat of grayish-red hair. Wang thought it was very ugly. No one seems to know what happened to the strange corpse.

Chinese scientists began to investigate. They were able to collect reports from over 100 people, who said they had seen the wildman. They also found strange, large footprints and hair samples.

In Europe there are also stories of a hairy wildman who lives deep in the forests or high in the mountains. The creature was supposed to be very strong and sometimes dangerously violent. Most of these stories of a European wildman are very old. There are no recent accounts of such a creature in Europe. If the European wildman did exist, it died out a long time ago.

None of this is solid proof of anything. As I have pointed out, stories are not concrete evidence. It could all be legend and rumor. But there are so many stories from so many different places, you have to wonder.

Perhaps some rare creature, either an unknown variety of ape or something halfway between man and ape, is hiding out in remote and desolate regions throughout the world. Some people think that there are several different species of wildman or apeman that remain yet to be discovered.

6

BIGFOOT: GOOD
NEWS, BAD NEWS

Over the last few years the Bigfoot
story has been like one of those good news,
bad news jokes. There have been some
encouraging signs. But there have been
discouraging ones too.

Let's get rid of some of the bad news first.

One of the most sensational stories in
Bigfoot history was the Ape Canyon "attack."
The "attack" was first reported in full in the
newspaper, the *Portland Oregonian,* for July
13, 1924.

The newspaper article told of how a group
of miners had gone prospecting on Mount St.

Helens in Washington State. Two of the miners spotted a Bigfoot-like creature. The miners called it a "giant ape." They took a shot at it and hit it. The "ape" fell off a cliff. That's why its body could not be recovered.

That night a group of five miners were in a cabin in a canyon. Suddenly a whole crowd of giant apes attacked the cabin. The apes showered the cabin with rocks and boulders. The miners were afraid to go out. One of them was knocked unconscious. But there were no serious injuries.

In the morning the miners crept out of their cabin. The apes were gone. Rocks and boulders were scattered around the cabin. There were also supposed to be giant ape-like footprints all around. The miners rushed to town. They returned with a lot of friends. Everybody was carrying a gun. No one fired a shot — because no one ever saw any giant apes.

Later, others reported finding giant prints in the same area. The place became known as Ape Canyon.

The Ape Canyon story is famous. It is retold in practically every Bigfoot book. Some people believed that the "apes" were Bigfoot creatures. But if there ever were any giant apes in Ape Canyon, they aren't there anymore. In 1980 Mount St. Helens, which is a volcano, erupted. The whole area around Ape Canyon was destroyed.

As far as Bigfoot is concerned there was worse to come. A retired logger has stepped forward and tried to destroy the whole Ape Canyon story. In 1982 Rant Mullens, 86 years old, told a Canadian newspaper that the Ape Canyon attack was all a hoax. Mullens said he and his uncle, George Ross, were the ones who had pulled off the hoax.

They were coming back from a fishing trip when they saw the miners' cabin. They decided to scare the miners. So in the evening they sneaked onto a ledge over the cabin. "George was always playing jokes," said Mullens. "He and I rolled some rocks down over the edge. Then we got out of there fast. When we heard the miners were telling hairy

107

ape stories, we both had a good laugh. We never told anyone the truth of the story."

Mullens didn't stop there. He said that a few years later he carved some huge wooden "feet." He used them to make footprints around some tourists' cars. When the tourists saw the footprints, says Mullens, "they got out of there fast."

At this point, Mullens says, he had enough of the joke. He put the feet away in a shed. But a friend found them. The friend used them to make footprints all over the area. A lot more people were scared.

In the 1940s, Mullens says, he whittled six more pairs of Bigfoot feet. He sold them to a man from California. The feet were then used to spread the Bigfoot legend throughout that state.

Mullens, who has lived in the Pacific Northwest his whole life, says, "I have never seen anything out there I could not explain." He doesn't think much of people who believe in Bigfoot. "Anyone who believes in Bigfoot has to be pretty narrow between the ears."

But some people who believe in Bigfoot don't believe Rant Mullens. Bigfoot believers certainly don't believe that Mullens and his uncle started the whole Bigfoot legend. They point out that he is a very old man, trying to remember things that happened over fifty years ago. There is no way to check the truth of this "confession." There were Bigfoot stories around even before Ape Canyon. And there are lots of sightings and photographs and other evidence that cannot be attributed to Mullens' carved feet.

Some Bigfoot hunters say that Mullens may have made up his whole story. Fred Beck, one of the miners who had originally told of the attack, talked to a lot of people before he died in the 1960s. Beck had always insisted that he was not fooled. He said the miners had not only seen footprints and heard the rocks falling on their cabin, they had seen the creatures themselves. Whose version of the events do you want to believe?

Grover Krantz, a Washington State University scientist who has studied Bigfoot, tends to believe Mullens. He thinks the whole Ape Canyon incident was a hoax. But Krantz also believes in Bigfoot. He had never put much faith in the miners' story. Krantz says it all sounded too sensational. No one else ever reported that the creatures traveled in large groups. And no one else reported that they were aggressive and did things like throw rocks at people. Practically all of the reports describe Bigfoot as shy and peaceful.

Krantz says that he is glad to get rid of the story. It just didn't fit in with the other evidence. But that hoax has no bearing on the rest of the Bigfoot evidence, he says.

So one Bigfoot case may—or may not—have been cleared up. At the very least it is more in doubt than it ever was.

Now for some good news. Good for those who want to believe that a large, unknown, hairy creature that walks on two legs is living in the Pacific Northwest, and perhaps in other parts of the country as well. The good news is that Bigfoot is still being seen. And Bigfoot—or something—is still leaving big strange-looking footprints. Here is a recent example.

On June 10, 1982, there was a very impressive Bigfoot "event" near Walla Walla, Washington. Paul Freeman, a U.S. Forest Service employee, was patrolling a wilderness area of the Blue Mountains near Walla Walla. Freeman got out of his truck and began to walk down an old logging road. Suddenly an "enormous creature" came through the bushes and stepped onto the road. It was about 200 feet in front of him. The thing was about eight feet tall, walked on two legs, had arms that dangled down to its knees, and was covered with reddish-brown fur. It also seemed to have a foul smell. It was a classic Bigfoot sighting.

Freeman eyed the creature. The creature eyed Freeman. Then they both decided to go off in opposite directions. They didn't want to tangle with one another. Freeman says he knows that what he saw wasn't a bear. And it wasn't a man in a gorilla suit. Whatever it was, it scared him badly. "I've never been

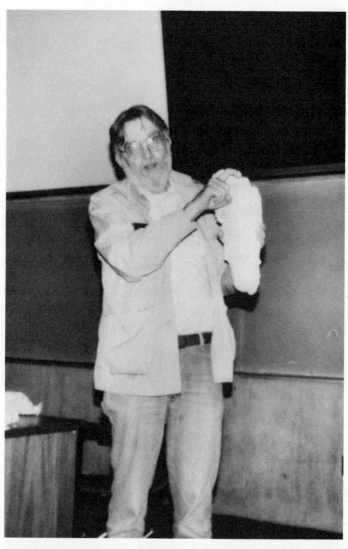

Dr. Grover Krantz holding cast of the Walla Walla Bigfoot print.

scared in the woods before. This thing was real. It was big enough to tear the head right off your shoulders." Freeman later said that just the thought of the thing was keeping him awake at night.

Freeman rushed back to his headquarters. He told others what he had seen. A couple of hours later a group of Forest Service employees returned to the area where Freeman had made his sighting. They found footprints, a trail of 21 of them. The prints were roughly human in shape, and very large. They measured 14 inches long by 7 inches wide.

The size of the prints was impressive enough. Even more impressive was their depth. The tracks were made on very hard ground. It was an old unpaved logging road. Yet the tracks were at least an inch deep. The heel part of the print was even deeper. It would take a lot of force to drive anything that deeply into hard ground. So if they were real footprints the thing that made them had to be very heavy and powerful.

The next day, June 11, a group headed by a man named Art Snow also reported seeing the prints. The group had been out searching the woods for a missing boy when they saw the trail. Snow said that they were able to follow the trail off into the woods for three-quarters of a mile. Snow said he didn't think the tracks were fake. "It would not be possible to fake the tracks without a helicopter... I'm not saying there is or is not a Bigfoot, but all the evidence verifies his [Freeman's] story."

About a week later Freeman and another ranger found a second set of strange tracks in the same general area. The Forest Service office brought in a professional tracker. The tracker looked at the second set of tracks, and decided that they were fake. Freeman disagreed. He thought the tracks were genuine. He said that the tracker was a professional at tracking people. But that he [Freeman] had been tracking animals for 30 years.

The controversy over the second set of

tracks did not affect Freeman's original sighting, or the tracks found in connection with it. But a controversy did develop even there.

Some Bigfoot supporters claimed that the Walla Walla "event" provided nearly conclusive proof that Bigfoot is real. Here is how they present their case. The man who sighted the creature worked for the U.S. Forest Service. He was an experienced outdoorsman and a reliable witness. The tracks were seen by other reliable witnesses.

Still, there is almost always a possibility that tracks can be faked. It might not have been easy to fake the tracks in the Walla Walla case, but it would have been possible. Everybody who has ever been seriously interested in Bigfoot knows that fake Bigfoot tracks have often been used to fool people. And sometimes these tracks have fooled people who should have known better.

Is it possible that someone was trying to fool Freeman? Perhaps. But remember, in addition to actually finding the tracks,

Freeman said that he also saw the thing that made the tracks. He didn't just catch a glimpse of it in the distance. He got a good look at it. He said that he could see the muscles of the creature's legs and shoulders moving under its fur. He was sure he could not be fooled.

So the theory that someone in a gorilla suit was running around in the woods trying to fool a Forest Service employee is pretty slim.

What it really comes down to is this: How reliable a witness was Paul Freeman? When evidence must depend on the word of a single witness, that can mean trouble. The Walla Walla Bigfoot sighting suffers from just that kind of trouble.

Some of the people who worked with Freeman insist that he was a perfectly ordinary and honest fellow. They say that he had never been particularly interested in Bigfoot. And that he seemed to have been really upset and frightened by what he had seen.

However, a Forest Service officer disagrees. He said that Freeman had been a "freak about Bigfoot. He talked about it all the time. I don't know whether he made the prints or someone else did it as a practical joke on him. But we're sure it was a hoax." He also pointed out that Freeman had only been a Forest Service employee for about a month before he made his sighting.

What did Freeman have to say about all of this? Not much. He quit the Forest Service in July, when his story began to get a lot of publicity. He hasn't been heard from since. And neither has the Walla Walla area Bigfoot.

Can we be sure the whole thing was a hoax? No, we can't. Freeman may just have gotten tired of people laughing at him, and calling him a faker. He may have figured the only thing he could do was get away from it all. You can hardly blame him. That has happened to a lot of people before.

But the Walla Walla "event" can't be used as solid evidence that Bigfoot exists either. It's another one of those good news, bad news stories.

Like so many other modern monster hunts,

the hunt for Bigfoot has been a frustrating one. It is probably more frustrating than any other modern monster hunt. People keep reporting that they see the thing. But the solid evidence never seems to be there.

Most of those who believe in Bigfoot still think that the creature is some kind of huge unknown ape. A few think it might be some kind of ape-man creature.

A small group has become so frustrated by Bigfoot's elusiveness that they are almost ready to give up. No, they won't say that Bigfoot doesn't exist. They think the creature is some sort of alien. A creature from another world. Or perhaps from another dimension or another reality. Bigfoot isn't really of this world, they say. That's why it's so hard to catch.

One of the leading spokesmen for this viewpoint is veteran monster hunter John Beckjord. Beckjord admits that most other monster hunters don't agree with him. "They think I'm some kind of nut," he says. Crypto-zoologists don't want to have anything to do

Veteran Bigfoot researcher Rene Dahinden with the cast of a Bigfoot print.

with people like Beckjord. They feel they have enough trouble getting scientists to listen to them.

Cryptozoologists are afraid that people like Beckjord who talk about aliens and beings from another dimension will just make a laughing stock out of cryptozoology. They say these theories turn science into science fiction. They wish that Beckjord and those who think like him would just go away and leave them alone.

In the meantime the less radical monster hunters still go out into the mountains and forests. They still follow up on reported sightings of Bigfoot. They study casts made of strange footprints. And they are sure that one day they will find Bigfoot, and it will be a real, solid, and earthly creature.

INDEX

121

DANIEL COHEN is a free-lance writer who has written numerous books for adults and young readers on subjects ranging from science to the supernatural. He is recognized as an authority on monsters, and is a charter member of the International Society of Cryptozoology, the organization of modern monster hunters who are trying to find and identify unknown creatures today.

Previous Cohen titles include *Ghostly Terrors, Creatures from UFOs, Science Fiction's Greatest Monsters, America's Very Own Monsters.*

Mr. Cohen is former managing editor of *Science Digest* magazine. He is a native of Chicago and holds a degree in journalism from the University of Illinois. He lives with his wife and daughter and a collection of cats and dogs in Port Jervis, New York.